Halloween Swear words

Halloween Coloring Book

Caitlyn Monroe concepts

Copyright (c) 2020 Caitlyn monroe

Shit is Real!

Here. Take my last fuck

Halloweed

FUCK NORMAL!

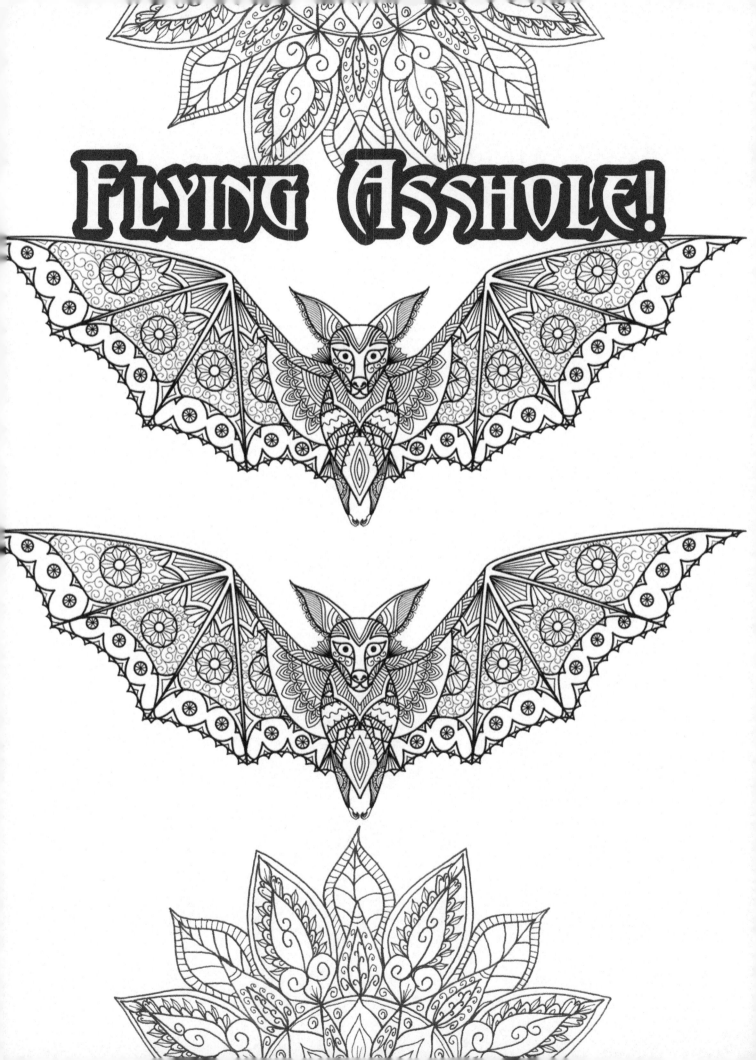

FLYING ASSHOLE!

BALL SUCKER!

Shit hole!

Made in United States
Orlando, FL
11 October 2022